IMAGES
of America

THE GATEWAY DISTRICT

John Eric's college days.

IMAGES
of America

THE GATEWAY DISTRICT

Shirley Pomeroy in conjunction with
Area Libraries and Historical Societies

First published 1997

ISBN 0-7524-0905-0

Published by Arcadia Publishing,
an imprint of the Chalford Publishing Corporation,
One Washington Center, Dover, New Hampshire 03820.
Printed in Great Britain

Library of Congress Cataloging-in-Publication Data applied for

The Huntington Public Library. Huntington's first library was established in 1855. Judge C.B. Huntington donated $100 to be used to establish a library in a store, which burned in 1859. The first board of trustees consisted of Patrick Hart, Edmund H. Cross, and H.J. Brown in 1893. James Gleason was the first librarian. Murrayfield School was used as the library in 1812. In 1930 the town built an extension onto the high school to house the library. The present library was built on that site.

Contents

Acknowledgments

The photographs in this volume have been borrowed from the collections in our town libraries and historical societies. Private collections were lent to the project by very generous neighbors: thanks to architect Jeffrey Scott Penn for his lovely collection of very early postcards; Nancy Eric; the Howes Brothers of Ashfield (A.W. and G.E.); Pam Donovan-Hall and Grace Wheeler from the Huntington Historical Society; and Alice Britton from Russell. Also thanks to Pam Anderson for collating and typing and to Alma LaFrance for helping to meet our deadline. My seven co-authors are as follows, and I am grateful for their participation: Helen Allyn, Montgomery; Karin Cook, Worthington; Fay Peirgiovanni and Rose Marie E. Healey-Picard, Chester; Pricilla Suriner, Middlefield; Connie Marshall Nichols, Blandford; and Catherine Moran, Russell.

Introduction

Welcome to a pictorial history of the Gateway District. This volume covers the years between 1760 and 1960.

The Gateway District is made up of seven historic towns located in western Massachusetts, and this pictorial and written history features each of those seven towns. Today, when local folks hear the term "The Gateway District," they immediately identify with seven specific hill towns that joined together in the creation of a regional school district. As you read through this book, you will see that the towns, while unique, share more than just a school system. There runs also a common thread of history and experience, and our photographic essay chronicles the lives of the area's people. In their earliest days, they shared a common industrial history of grist and sawmills, charcoal kilns, cider mills, meetinghouses, and one-room schools. Basket and wood-turning skills became family enterprises, as did the scythe-stone and soap-stone quarries. Agricultural interests included farming, selling firewood, stock-raising, and the making of maple sugar and cheese. The Boston and Albany Railroad brought with it a different kind of industry. Fabric and paper mills developed, then declined. By 1960 the era had ended.

Welcome and enjoy. Town libraries and historical societies as well as private individuals have generously lent to our project, which we are sure will be treasured by generations to come.

One
Town of Chester

The land grant known as Township #9 included what is now the Town of Chester. The original proprietors were John Murray, Abijah Willard, Timothy Paine, and John Chandler. In January of 1763, a meeting was held to admit more settlers (there were nineteen thus far). A time frame was set for the fencing, tilling, home construction, and actual settlement of families upon the land. Thus, settlement began in the area of Chester Center, where many farms sit high on the hill. Also settled were North Chester, Dayville, and Littleville, because of their ability to provide waterpower via the middle branch of the Westfield River, then called the Agawam River, for the operation of sawmills, gristmills, and other enterprises.

Chester Factory Village developed as the economic center later, when many mineral deposits were mined and with the coming of the Great Western Railroad. Industry developed along the west branch of the Westfield River, which provided waterpower and was conveniently located near the railroad.

Mineral-related operations flourished in Chester Factory Village from the mid-1800s to the mid-1900s. The high quality of the emery, mica, and granite of the area are known worldwide.

Chester remains a place of bucolic vistas, cool forests, and sparkling waters that draws many a visitor to the area.

Chester Factory Village looking southeast. Nestled in the river valley and encompassed by hills, the entire village area, with William Street in the foreground, is depicted in this photograph.

The Cushman Tavern, built around 1770 by Thomas Elder and his son James. The tavern features hand-hewn beams and a large stone fireplace and was quite spacious for its day. The third owner was Mr. Cushman, for whom it is now named. The tavern also served as the North Chester Post Office from 1888-1925. Local legend purports that George Washington stopped here on his trip to Boston.

North Chester c. 1800. Known as the Little House, this one-and-a-half story colonial has distinctive, nine-pane "eyebrow" windows.

The Zenas Searles house on Skyline Trail. Built in 1787, the Searles house is one of the original Federal saltbox styles. It still retains its hand-hewn beams, witches' stairway, twelve-over-twelve windows on the first floor, and eight-over-eight windows on the second floor.

North Chester schoolhouse. Built in 1850 and the only other schoolhouse left in town, this building served the students of North Chester until 1920. School districts were enacted in 1779, with each designated schoolhouse not to exceed 20 by 18 feet in area!

The First Congregational Church in Chester Center, built in 1835. It is an exact copy of one built in New Marlborough, Massachusetts, by architect Henry A. Sykes. Timber from the first meetinghouse—which dated from 1769—was used in its construction, all boards numbered for ease of reuse.

The Second Congregational United Church in Chester Factory Village, built in 1843. This is a Greek Revival style church with modest ornamentation. It serves as a focal point when entering the village from the west.

DeWitt Clinton DeWolf and daughter Virginia, *c.* 1900. DeWolf, a prominent lawyer and secretary to the governor, purchased the Erastus Pease home on Chester Hill in 1872.

The butcher shops of River Street. The delivery wagons of the River Street Market and T. Smithies are shown here. Though the building resembles a home, there is a butchers' hoist and exterior cooler door on the second floor.

The first five of ten Peirgiovanni children, *c.* 1925. From left to right are Rosena, Louisa, Margaret, Dalfina, and Mary.

Chester Center School. Built in 1796, the Chester Center School is the oldest remaining schoolhouse in town and is largely intact. The first headmaster was Deacon Parmeter, who had a long affiliation with the education of Chester children. Another early educator was David Shepard Jr.

A late 1800s family portrait that was found in a Chester barn. Do you know who this austere and somber family might be?

The Senter family, late 1800s. Charles and Catherine Senter are seen with their children, Kim, Ann, Ed, John, and Olive.

Welcome Home! The Chester Factory Village's Fay building is seen here all decked out in bunting.

Early 1900s at the Riverside Inn. There once were livery barns across the street from the hotel. Don't you wonder what this men's gathering was about? Who's that woman on the upper porch? Note the automobile's buttoned upholstery and the driver's goggles!

Victorian style, c. 1890. This photograph was found in the attic of the Willcutt building. Unfortunately, it isn't labeled.

Right out of the Old West! The Willcutt building housed a barbershop and other conveniences of the day. Shown c. 1900 with full first- and second-floor porches and shuttered windows, it is currently known as the Longhorn Saloon.

E.H. Alvord's Blacksmith Shop, 1915. Chester native Edwin Henry Alvord ran away to sea as a young teen. He was to have captained a ship, but his mother convinced him to return home. Thence he was "bound out" to a blacksmith. Eventually he opened his own shop on North Main Street and built the house, barn, and two cottages that stand across the street from the shop location. He also was a deputy sheriff in Hampden and Berkshire Counties for forty-one years.

The Battels family home on Emery Street. Ann and Mary Battels appear with their brother in front of their "Irish Shanty" home. Built in 1841 when the Irish rail workers set up camp, this shanty was one of the last of "The Patch" to remain. "The Patch" filled what is now the ball field area of Emery Street.

A public necessity! A horse trough was located at the corner of Middlefield Street and Jacob's Ladder Trail.

Chester's first baseball team, 1901. Team members were James Harrington, Jay Ripley, Walter Parker, Connie Harrington, Gordon Mead, Fred Moulton, Charlie Harrington, Dan Luce, and Bill Haley.

Just hangin' around. Shown here *c.* 1920 are Arthur O. Wilander, Walter Piispanen, Edwin Wilander, and girls.

Ernie "Junie" Pike and his team of oxen were a frequent sight at the Littleville Fair in 1945.

The switchboard operators. Chief Operator Pat Ripley appears with her team, Mary Jacobson, Rita Wiley, Guida Jacobson, Ginny Hunt DeSanto, and Nettie Leighton.

Making switches for the Finnish Saunas. The Finnish steam baths were a popular cultural aspect of life in Chester as late as the 1940s. Here Maria Wilander, Aino Luoto, Vieno Luoto Leone, and Thomas Luoto are shown making the switches.

Railroad history. The Chester Depot appears here in 1843.

The mica mill workers who processed sheets of mica into isinglass for wood stove doors. They also made low voltage insulators with mica.

The former Chester High School in Chester Factory Village, built in 1923. Prior to educational regionalization, this housed the high school. It is now home to Chester Commons elder housing.

The Chester Elementary School, built in 1908. The building shows its Romanesque influence in arched windows and a semicircular fan light over the main entrance. The clock was provided by the fund-raising efforts of Geneva M. Burleigh, an eighth-grade student at the time, for a sum of $345. During the early 1900s, the New York School of Fine and Applied Arts held summer sessions here.

St. John's Roman Catholic Church. Dedicated in 1915, this house of worship served the needs of the growing Italian and Irish populations.

The old jail. A need for this unique hill town building came about with the coming of the Western Railroad. The rough-and-tumble rail construction crews and illegal train passengers sometimes caused some mayhem in downtown. The building now houses the historical society.

Railroad history: August 31, 1893. The Great Chester Train Wreck caused a tangle of steel!

Eastman's Sawmill in Littleville. The dam and mill were constructed in 1764 when Huntington was part of Chester. The mill served as a gristmill as well as a lumber sawing operation over the years.

Two

Town of Russell

Russell is one of the small hill towns nestled in the foothills of the Berkshires. The town is made up of three distinct villages joined by the Westfield River. It is no coincidence that Woronoco, Russell Village, and Cresent Mills were each built up near a mill on the river at the same period as the railroad came through (1841). The railroad made access to the tremendous waterpower possible.

New immigrants to the United States were a boon to the industrial development in Russell. The early settlement near Hazard Pond, now known as Russell Pond, survives as only a ghost of what it once was. The Industrial Revolution changed the town from an isolated agrarian community with small lumber and gristmills to a prosperous town with jobs for all.

In recent years, Russell has seen the decline of the importance of the mills to the economic well-being of its residents. The Westfield River Paper Company and Number 1 Mill at International Paper both closed, and fewer Russell residents depend on the mills for employment. Russell is changing again. In many ways it has become a suburb of Westfield, yet it clings to its association with the other hill towns. It is a special place where the hills are higher, the air is cooler, the rocks are more plentiful, and the people truly care about their neighbors. As you read this chapter about Russell, keep in mind how it came to be and that it was the people who chose to live here that made it so.

Home of William and Sylvia Cortis, *c.* 1871. The Cortis family was one of the earliest to settle "on the mountain" in Russell in the vicinity of Route 23. The earliest settlers made their homes in the Hazard Pond area (Russell Pond), along what would be known as the General Knox Trail.

Virginia Forish and her father. The Forishes were another family that lived "on the mountain." Elizabeth, the younger sister of Virginia, does not ever remember her father without his gun.

Main Street, *c.* 1910. Russell was famed for its tree-lined Main Street, now listed in the National Register of Historic Places. Today, the view down Main Street doesn't look much different, with the exception of automobile's supplanting the horse and buggy.

Charcoal kilns. The smell of charcoal kilns gave Russell the nickname of "Stink Town" at one time. Mount Shatterack is the backdrop for the Russell Depot in its original location on east side of the Westfield River. The old iron bridge was wiped out by ice dams in the early 1900s.

Ferry across the Westfield River. Using Yankee ingenuity, the residents of Russell didn't let an ice jam restrict their access to the train depot on the other side of the river. A rope was strung across the river to guide the course of the ferry. Jack Smith is at the helm. A new bridge was built in 1910.

Boyden House. Minnie Boyden and her family are seen in front of Boyden House on Main Street about 1900. The building later became the Ford Inn, a boarding house with a bunk house on the second floor. (Alice Britton Collection.)

Rogers' Store, 1900. Floyd Hibert, Charles Peckham, Ernest "Pop" DeCoteau, and Tom Rogers stand in front of the general store, which was also the home of the post office.

The Russell House. This old hotel on Main Street was built around the time the railroad came through Russell in 1841. A short walk from Russell's depot, with gambling, a "men's only" bar, and other attractions, the hotel attracted clientele from Westfield and Springfield. It was the sight of many local weddings and banquets for years. The town was well housed in the "tank room" in the hotel. Around 1930 it became a rooming house. Today an apartment house, it doesn't look much different that it did in its prime. (Edwin Larrabee collection.)

Gridley's Store, Main Street (next to the Community church). The store is decked out in red, white, and blue to welcome home World War I veterans. It became Martin's Boarding House and later was divided into apartments. Russell's Barber Shop was located in this building. (Alice Britton Collection.)

Old Trolley Bridge. Fred Martin and Ed Parks stand near an abandoned trolley bridge across Black Brook (behind Red Men's Hall). The wooden part of the bridge was destroyed by a July Fourth fire set by local youths. A buyer was found, and the state moved the bridge to Tolland State Forest, where it is still in use today. (Alice Britton Collection.)

Swinging Bridge. A footbridge connected "The Grove" to Lincoln Street. The workers at the Westfield River Paper Company who lived on Grove Street used this bridge to get to work, enabling them to go home at noon to eat. A factory whistle regulated the lives of most of the residents of this section of Russell.

Choir at Woronoco Hall, 1895. Reverend Van Allen was the pastor and Miss Lottie Stearns was the organist. (Alice Britton Collection.)

Old age and youth. "Uncle Bill" Mortimer appears here with his youngest lamb. This 1906 photograph taken in front of Mortimer Homestead on Route 20 was taken from a booklet called *The Scenic Trolley Route of New England* put out by the Western Massachusetts Street Railway. Grazing sheep at this farm were one the tour's highlights.

Russell school on Blandford Stage Road, c. 1907. Russell operated several small schools throughout the town for many years; this one housed grades one and two. As roads improved, children began to go to larger schools that were centrally located. Harvey Clark saved this school photograph. He is the wet, barefoot boy second from the right. From appearances, he was not the only student who didn't go directly to school.

Graduating class of Russell school about 1900. Shown here are Mrs. Wager, Russell Tower, Aldea DeCoteau, Ruth (Cowles) Stein, and Charles Cook. (Alice Britton Collection.)

Russell Elementary School teachers, *c.* 1934. Most Russell residents "of a certain age" remember Miss Cavanaugh, Miss Victory, Stanley Everett, Mrs. Bronson, and Mrs. Wager.

George Washington Frost. Russell's last Civil War veteran tried to sign up three times while he was too young; he was finally able to enlist at age nineteen. According to research done by Louise Mason, "He was a farmer, Civil War volunteer, homesteader in the West, osteopath and healer, herbalist, psychic and teller of tales." For over thirty years, Mr. Frost visited the Russell and Woronoco schools on Memorial Day and told tales of his Civil War adventures. He died in 1949 at age ninety-eight.

Lavinia Parks Culver on the occasion of her 100th birthday.

Russell Community Church. The white church was built in 1853 by a Baptist congregation and was later joined by the Methodists. The church has continued as an independent church and is an integral part of Russell life.

Our Lady of the Rosary. The brown church serves parishioners from Russell, Blandford, and Montgomery. Catholic services were held in a barn, at Blandford State Road School, at the town hall, and even at the "casino" in Woronoco until the present church was built in 1927. Two old chalices recently found in what was formerly Gaulberti's barn were probably from the period before the church was built. (PVPC.)

Russell Package Store. Standard Oil owned this business run by Mr. Andre Jamellier in 1927. In 1974 the building was purchased by John Pappas and has been run as the Russell Package Store since that time. (Alice Britton Collection.)

Russell Inn, *c*. 1930. Mrs. Lydia Jamellier is in front of what was once Russell school. A second floor was added to offer tourist rooms. (Alice Britton Collection.)

Great Falls of Westfield River. Cyrus W. Field used this representation of the Great Falls in an advertisement for the sale of the property in 1843. The advertisement read, "20 miles from Springfield, 4 hours by train to Albany, 6 to Boston, and 9 to New York. 30-40 foot falls, rail access, enough water for three 'largest class' cotton mills. Bed and bank of river of white coarse granite and slate rock." Cyrus Field used the proceeds from the sale to finance the laying of the trans-Atlantic cable that linked America and Europe electronically.

Chapin and Gould. In 1858 Chapin and Gould purchased this site and built a paper mill. The falls at Crescent Mills was a perfect spot to take advantage of the hydropower of the river and the plentiful supply of water. Texon, maker of industrial fiberboard (the type used for athletic shoe insoles, among other applications), now operates this site. (Alice Britton Collection.)

Vernon Paper Company at Salmon Falls, 1870s. In 1905 Horace Moses purchased the property and opened Strathmore Paper Company, which is known worldwide as a maker of premium printing and artist stock and bonded writing papers.

Rag picking room at Westfield River Paper Company. Many of the residents of Russell were originally attracted to the area by the job opportunities afforded by the three paper mills along the Westfield River. Up until several years ago, Westfield River Paper Company was one of the primary makers of glassine paper in the country.

Horace A. Moses, founder of Strathmore Paper Company. He understood that the physical, mental, and spiritual well being of his workers was important. Woronoco became a model community with a community center, its own dairy herd, school, modern housing, and the personal interest Horace Moses took in his employees. After his death in 1947, the vision of a harmonious community with Strathmore Paper Company at its center gradually faded. He was founder of Eastern States Exposition, Junior Achievement, Inc., and the Hampden County Improvement League. (Joan Gorman Sheehan.)

Twenty-five Year Club. Westfield River Paper Company honored its Twenty-five Year Club members at a dinner at the Strathmore Inn in Woronoco in February 1925. From left to right are as follows: (front row) Frank Helms, Evie Allen, Bea Morreau, Fred Newton, Paul Moore, and Frank Welch; (row 2) Bill Perry, Francis Bull, Jim Castro, Jimmy Falvo, Cornielius Paetzel, Paul Paetzel, Louis Dame, and Howard Thayer; (row 3) Frank Hathaway, unknown, Ernest Church, Sammy Green, Bill Churchill, Henry Cowles, Chenier, unknown, and Burt Cook; (row 4) Ray Bull, Charlie Cook, Sammy Greene, Louis Dosier, Leroy Frisbee, "Johnny" Gordon Reed, and Harold Marcotte; (back row) Al Moultenbry, Mr. Castell, unknown, Morris Losier, Sam Rovard, Joe Glasing, Frank Morninghoff, Harry Ford, Louis Crawford, Andy Feustel, and unknown.

Shooting hoops. The Outing Club sponsored Russell's town basketball team in 1924. Mr. Higgins, Pete Regan, Mr. Beaureguard, Mr. Bush, Pete Daurin, Marty Fouche, "Bum" Ellis, and Roy Bull are pictured here. Ski jumping on Pine Hill was another popular Outing Club activity.

Girls basketball team, 1950. The upstairs at the Russell Town Hall was the scene of many town activities including plays, concerts, parties, and basketball games. From left to right are (front row) Connie Thayer Herman, Elaine DeCoteau Gamble, Shirley Cook Wheeler, Catherine Langlois Frink, Flory Boyden, and Lillian LaBombard; (back row) Maryanne Zielenski Pratt, Lois Weheley Bednarski, Mrs. Josephine Abnerathy, Shirley Smith Porter, Jo-Ann Britton, and Connie Curro Lane.

Russell Volunteer Fire Department. A tired Bill Chadwick is seen on Main Street in Russell. When the fire horn blew, men working at paper mills dropped what they were doing to respond to the call. Today, Russell still relies on its volunteer fire department, but no longer can we depend on mill workers alone. Instead, electronic beepers call locals to aid their town.

Flood of 1955. Fortuna Sharkey and sons Pat and Mickey are walking down what is left of Main Street. The Town of Russell was virtually cut off from the rest of the world after the flood washed out most roads, phone service, and electric power.

Train wreck. In 1948 there was a train wreck in the vicinity of Westfield River Paper Company. These tracks were part of a very busy corridor, hauling goods and passengers from Boston to Albany.

Russell Welcome Home Day. In 1919 Russell held a huge celebration to welcome home its veterans and honor those who fought in World War I, including Chauncy Walker, who gave his life for his country in that war.

Three

Town of Montgomery

Montgomery was incorporated as a town on November 28, 1780, during the stormiest days of the Revolution. The town was named in honor of General Richard Montgomery, who was killed during the siege of Quebec in 1776.

Although Montgomery is the third smallest town in the Commonwealth and the smallest of the hill towns, its peaceful country landscape offers a quiet refuge from larger surrounding communities.

This rural, residential town is nestled 1,050 feet above sea level at the town center. It is in Hampden County and bordered on the north by Huntington, to the south by the city of Westfield, on the west by Russell, and to the east by Southampton. It is situated in the Berkshire foothills and is easily accessible to major transportation highways in the area.

Montgomery was first settled in 1767 and until fairly recently was a farming community. There is no industry, but there are a few small home businesses consisting of construction equipment companies, local artisans, family daycare homes, and the Mountain View Nursing Home. The children of Montgomery are students of the Gateway Regional School District.

A friendly community, Montgomery offers an escape to a quieter time with miles of wooded areas to hike, scenic views, and small mountain streams, which offer some fine fishing.

The Main Road from Montgomery to Westfield in the late 1800s.

Hurricane Diane. Nearly 26 inches of rain from this August 1955 storm severely damaged the Main Road near the Montgomery-Westfield town line.

The Danek-Zolatz home on Main Road. Formerly owned by Henry Stiles, it is presently owned by the Cruikshank family.

The Captain John Hildreth House. Called the Owl's Nest, it was built about 1800 by Elisha Chapman and is presently owned by Joan Fox.

The David Allyn homestead on Main Road. Originally the Old Chapman Tavern, this building is no longer standing. The Montgomery Volunteer Fire Department is now located where it stood.

John Camp's place on Main Road, built between 1830 and 1850. It is currently the home of the Otis family.

The Roland Avery house on Avery Road. Roland and Nancy Avery are on the front lawn along with a friend. The house is currently owned by Mr. and Mrs. Harold Avery.

One of the last farms in Montgomery, which was owned by the Danek-Zolatz families.

The Montgomery Corner School. This was the last one-room district school in Montgomery and it closed in the early 1950s.

The Montgomery Community Church, shown here with the Montgomery Historical Building. The church was built in 1797 and the historical building in 1849.

The Montgomery Town Hall's new wing. The original town hall was built in 1849, and the addition was finished in the spring of 1997. It includes the new library, town offices, and a senior room.

C. Clinton Clark with "Major." The two appear in the dooryard of the F.W. Clark home on Main Road.

Sand Knoll Cemetery, one of the oldest cemeteries in town.

The old balcony in the Montgomery Town Hall. This was removed in the early 1950s when the building was renovated.

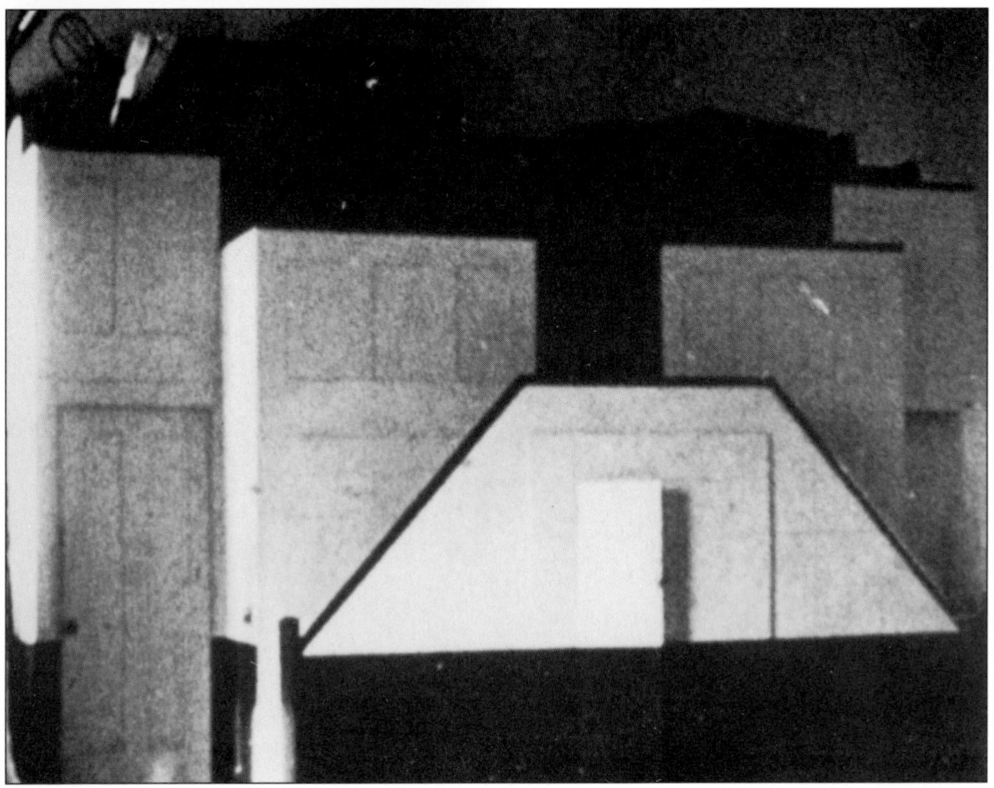

Faye Clark with "Chub" on Main Road.

A 1912 hayride for the guests at Moore's Mountain House.

The old barn across the road from the Mountain House on Mountain House Road. Many good times, square dances, husking bees, etc. were enjoyed here.

The Crescent Dairy truck owned by Sharon Williston.

The 1913 Montgomery Baseball Team. From left to right are (front row) Ray Manley, Perley Manley, Fred Williams, and Seth Bull; (back row) Lester Moore, Alfred Martin, Milo Cushman, Charlie Martin, and unknown.

New state school on June 8, 1917. From left to right are (front row) May Sporbert, Dexter Phillips, and Gertrude Sporbert; (back row) Raymond Avery, Harold Avery, Louis Sporbert, Stanley Camp, and Leslie Camp. The teacher is Grace (Sumner) Hall.

Park Chapman as a young boy.

Celestia (Chapman) Avery when she was a young girl.

Wilber Moore and his wife, the former Martha Stowell, on their wedding day in 1894.

Children of Edson and Lena Washburn in 1934. From left to right are Betty, Arlene, George, and Barbara. Gerald and Gene are in front.

The children of Bill and Grace Hall with their coonhounds. From left to right are Peggy, June, and Bill Hall Jr.

Pitcher Street School about 1898. Nellie Knight is the teacher of this class.

Helen Allyn appears next to English Grass Cave in Montgomery in 1954.

A pastoral scene—Homer Kelso with his oxen on New State Road.

Montgomery Thimble Club in the late 1920s. This photograph was taken in the front yard of the Camp home on Main Road. From left to right are (front row) Esther Kelso, Edith Kelso, Francis Feldman, Minnie Camp, and Mildred Bartlett; (middle row) Mary Herrick and Ruth Kelso; (back row) Gussie Williams, unknown, Bertha Camp, Mabel Kelso, Maude Allyn, Mrs. Feldman, Isabel Knox, Helen Kelso, and Alice Carter.

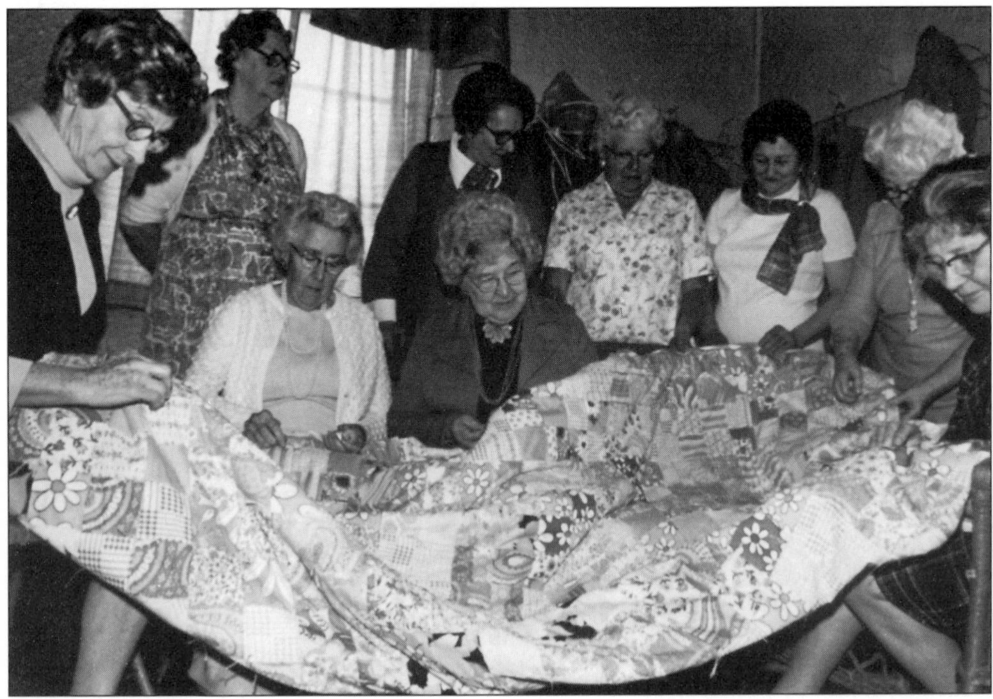

Montgomery Thimble Club working on a quilt. From left to right are (front row) Celestia Avery, Belle Grant, and unknown; (back row) Hazel Church, Frona Camp, Leah Edwards, Mary Leonard, Doris Giguere Blair, and Phyllis Royal.

Teacher Susan (Ondras) Allyn with her class on a field trip. From left to right are (front row) Arlene Washburn, Verna Szarek, and Edwina Brach; (middle row) George Washburn, Esther McQuat, unknown, unknown, unknown, and Susan (Ondras) Allyn; (back row) Betty Washburn, Peggy Hall, unknown, and Dottie Hall.

Montgomery schoolchildren from the Corner School performing in the Montgomery church. From left to right are (front row) Susan Gaunt, Sandy Spencer, Bobby Nesin, Mary Ellen Camp, Phillip Camp, Edna Avery, Donnie Camp, and Judy Nesin; (second row) Jimmy Gaunt, Richard Chapman, Leslie Camp, Lorna Camp, Georgianna Butman, Helen Allyn, Betty Ann Camp, Pat Howland, Robert Howland, Eddie Chapman, and Jerry Spencer; (third row) Joyce Chapman, Jennie Butman, music teacher Audria Albro, superintendent of schools Dana Webber, Ann Allyn. teacher Dorothy Laughlin, Kay Chapman, and Harold Butman.

Teacher Alvah Rhines with his class on a field trip in the late 1940s. From left to right are (front row) Florence Butman, Mary Ellen Camp, Edna Avery, and Betty Ann Camp; (middle row) Kay Chapman, Charlie Chase, Leslie Camp, Joyce Chapman, Eddie Helms, Elizabeth Helms, Ann Allyn, Jennie Butman, Richard Chapman, Harold Butman, Helen Allyn, and Roland Avery; (back row) Barbara Camp, Richard Avery, and Mr. Alvah Rhines.

The Montgomery Republican Committee in Washington, DC, with Vice President Richard Nixon. From left to right are Eunice (Dinty) Spencer, Gerald Spencer, Isabel Camp, John Camp, Richard Nixon, Frona Camp, Raymond Avery, Wesley Monat, and Milo Cushman.

Four

Town of Worthington

Worthington, a part of the western Hampshire Highlands, was purchased from the Massachusetts Bay Province as Plantation No. 3 in 1762. It was settled by 1764, incorporated as a town in 1768, and named for Colonel John Worthington, one of the five plantation owners. One of its early roads became part of the route between Boston and Albany. General Lafayette followed it in 1825 when he made his historic visit to Worthington on his way to the dedication of Bunker Hill.

The community has always been rural with an interest in agriculture, and this remains true today. Small-scale farming, maple syrup production, logging, and outdoor recreation appeal to residents. Throughout the past two centuries there have been cottage industries. Over time, tanneries and gristmills have been replaced by electronics enterprises and construction companies. Auto repair shops and herbal product stores have taken the place of the old factories. Travelers now spend the night in bed and breakfasts instead of a large hotel. Restaurants and taverns remain.

In recent times Worthington has made a subtle lifestyle shift, becoming a community with more of its residents traveling to larger surrounding cities for employment and entertainment. Both the Worthington Grange and the Women's Benevolent Society dissolved in the 1990s as people focused on activities outside of town.

While the hillsides that were bare not long ago are covered again with trees, the town continues in many ways as it always has. Fires and even deaths have brought no major change to Worthington. Town Meeting, held the first Saturday in May, provides an opportunity for all to participate in democracy. There is no railroad and, until recently, it was difficult traveling here by car; this has perhaps been a blessing. Those who live in Worthington see it as a special place a little bit removed from the rest of the world.

Acknowledgments: The committee who worked together to produce the Worthington section of this book was comprised of Bee Smith, Ted Porter, Helen Magargal, Elodi McBride, and Karin Cook. The names of all those who loaned photographs are noted in the appropriate places. Thanks go to all who participated. Without their cooperation this project would not have been possible.

Worthington about 1900. Alice and Marion Bartlett are walking west on what is now Routes 143 and 112 toward the Worthington Inn and the corners. In the distance is the hillside that would become the golf course. (Photograph property of Helen Magargal.)

Housecleaning c. 1900. Ladies well-dressed for housecleaning take a midmorning break on the wall in front of The Spruces, the Bartlett-Magargal home. (Photograph property of Helen Magargal.)

Mrs. Tufts. This artist who lived on Buffington Hill Road is seen here painting a landscape around 1900. (Photograph property of Helen Magargal.)

Young oxen and boys. Frank Burr is in the cart and Dan Porter is in charge. This is how the house on the corner of Sam Hill Road and Route 112 looked in 1913. The porch has since been removed but the second-story gabled windows remain. The house is presently the home of the Andersens. (Photograph property of Helen Magargal.)

Ice harvesting. Electricity came to Worthington in the 1920s. Before then ice was needed for refrigeration. Here it is being harvested for iceboxes and ice sheds by Arthur Pomeroy (left) and Louis Zarr (right). (Photograph property of Ted Porter.)

Lester LeDuc of Chesterfield in 1923. Lester is on his way up Randall's (Mason's) Hill to visit his future bride, Alice Bartlett. There is no pavement on The Williamsburg Road. (Photograph property of Helen Magargal.)

A vintage auto. This Model A was pulled from a snow bank by Herbert G. Porter and his horse in the late 1920s. (Photograph property of Ted Porter.)

Storm recovery. A 10-ton tractor from Hinsdale opened the roads in Worthington in 1945. (Photograph property of Helen Magargal.)

Seasonal hardships. Snow and ice storms have always been part of Worthington winters. This photograph of Lafayette Lodge was taken after 1916. The first hotel on this site was Bartlett's Hotel (built in 1858). It burned in 1898 and was replaced with the Worthington Inn. When it was sold, the new owners named it Lafayette Lodge. It burned down in 1936. Eventually Henry Snyder's home, Brickhaven, was built on this site. It is now owned by Vickie and Wayne Fisk. (Photograph property of Ted Porter.)

Hurricane-related floods in 1938. Here on Route 112 with the Capen-Riverside School in the background, Merwin "Stub" Packard, owner of the Corners Grocery, distributed ice cream much to the interest of Charlie Bartlett. The electricity was out and frozen items were given away to those who worked replacing the bridge. Gravel was dug from what is now Gugnoni's land and moved with Dan Porter's dump truck to rebuild the roadbed. Others brought planks and two-man saws to cut hemlock from the woods nearby, making it possible for the milk truck to get through. (Photograph property of Cullen "Pete" Packard.)

An ingenious solution. When there was no electricity at the Corners Grocery, Merwin "Stub" Packard devised a hand pump from a bicycle wheel to enable him to pump gas. (Photograph property of Cullen "Pete" Packard.)

A Plumb Ax Company cutting demonstration across from the Corners Grocery on the Torrey lawn in the late 1930s. The story is still told in 1997 that this company man was discovered using an ax that was not a Plumb. In the crowd were George Brown (in the felt hat at center rear) and Peter McEwan (to the right of Brown, wearing a V-neck shirt). Seated on the log at right were Louis Zarr (left) and Daniel Porter (right). (Photograph property of Cullen "Pete" Packard.)

Farm chores. In the 1940s, farming was still a way of life for many families. Here Archer Fitzgerald pitches hay up to Dan Porter. (Photograph property of Harriet Burr.)

Wilber Eddy driving Fred and Jerry to Dan Porter's sawmill on McCann land. This was before the time of skidders, cherry pickers, and logging trucks. (Photograph property of Ted Porter.)

Dan Porter and Earl Robinson sawing lumber. The sawyer sold some of the lumber at the site to the people in town. Hardwood cut to specific dimensions was purchased for railroad ties by Marshall Siebold in Westfield and Northampton. A company in Irving, Massachusetts, bought sugar maple for shoe heels. This photograph was taken in 1951 by Roy McCann. (Photograph property of Ted Porter.)

The Royal Order of the Buzzards. Entertainment did not always mean a trip to Northampton for dinner, driving to the mall, or renting a video. This photograph of a buzzards' social gathering shows Guy Thrasher, Walter Fox, and Dan Porter enjoying a night out at what had been the Manley Stetson house, owned then by Fred Emerson. Fred Emerson took the photograph probably in the late 1940s. (Photograph property of Ted Porter.)

Oat-thrashing machine, last used *c.* 1940. Oats were grown as horse feed on either the large field at the Porters' on Sam Hill Road or at the McCanns' on Old North Road. From left to right are (front row) Dan Porter, Arthur Pomeroy, and Vernon "Joe" Beals; (back row) David McEwan, Wilbur Eddy, Charles "Chuck" Eddy, and Carl Pomeroy. (Photograph property of Ted Porter.)

Swearing in. The honors are conducted at the 1952 Town Meeting by Town Clerk Franklin H. Burr, inducting the almoners of the Whiting Street Fund: Herbert Porter, Ernest Thayer, and Fordyce Knapp. These men were all in their eighties and had held their positions for over thirty years. (Photograph property of Harriett Burr.)

View c. 1947. This image looks toward the First Congregational Church through a Gothic snow arch, one of many created by Emerson Davis when he was custodian of the church. (Photograph property of Helen Magargal.)

A quilting bee. Church members and supporters, together with the Women's Benevolent Society, piece together a quilt about sixty years ago at the home of Edith Gurney Brewster on Harvey Road (the house is now owned by Bob Broderick). From left to right are Jessie Brewster, Mae Kilbourn, Mary Smith, Bessie Ames, Carmelita Martin, Mary Smart, Irene Porter, Flora Russell, Josephine Hewitt, and May Gurney Porter. (Photograph property of Ted Porter.)

Meeting of the Women's Benevolent Society, 1940s. This meeting took place at the home of Mrs. Harry Bates (located on Buffington Hill Road and now owned by Jeffrey and Dolores Racz). Florence was a very caring nurse who was the driving force behind the creation of the Worthington Medical Center. Her husband played piano, fiddle, and banjo. His small band, the Bates Orchestra, provided music for events at Lyceum Hall. Harry was also a very competent carpenter and stone mason: he built the fireplace on the stage of the town hall. (Photograph property of Ted Porter.)

Characters in a 1944 church play. Some possible identities, using the married names of the girls, are Bee Fairman Smith, Lucy Mollison (in beard), Dan Porter III and Ted Porter (sitting together on the lawn), Ernie Robinson, Edith Synder Packard, Shirley Robinson Sampson, and Phyllis Packard Eddy. (Photograph property of Ted Porter.)

Milking time. Mary Lou Osgood Dragon milks the cow her dad, Ken, kept in a garage near the corners in the late 1940s. (Photograph property of Helen Magargal.)

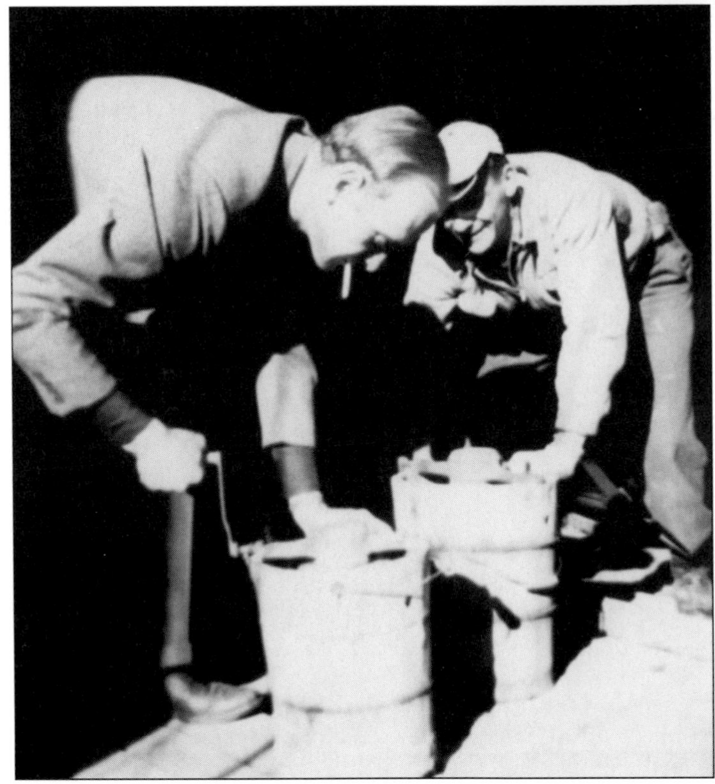

A pleasant dairy chore. Putting cream to use, brothers "Bevo" Horace and George Bartlett make ice cream for a big family reunion. (Photograph property of Helen Magargal.)

Play ball! Before there was a ball field at the rod and gun club, baseball was played in a lot on Old Post Road, past what is now the Jalberts' house. These players were all sponsored by local businesses. The date is remembered as 1948, 1949, or 1950. Standing in front of the Landa home (owned last by Jean and Larry Burnham) are (front row) Richard Sanderson, Sonny Ducharme, John Diamond, unknown, unknown, Grant Knapp (?), and Jackie Tinker; (middle row) Eugene Sawyer, George Bergin, "Bam" Warren Packard, Richard Fairman, Ted Porter, Howard Pease, and Harley Mason; (back row) Joe Landa (police chief and team organizer) and Constable Bob Nelson (at the other end of the flag). The coach, Ray Magargal, is kneeling in front with the team's mascot, Bub Hathaway (?). (Photographs property of Helen Magargal.)

Harvest season. Ben Albert, owner of Albert's Farms, and Henry Dassetti, his foreman (left), admire the crop in 1950. (Photograph property of Aida Albert.)

No small potatoes. By 1962 growing potatoes was big business for Albert's Farms. Here Bert Nugent operated a mechanical picker with Ken Beach at his side. (Permission to use this photograph has been granted by the *Springfield Sunday Republican*. The image was loaned to this project by Aida Albert.)

Clearing the fairway. The Worthington Golf Club was organized in 1904. Here, Spencer Parish of West Worthington moves a stone with what was reputed to be the town's strongest team of horses. This stone did not go too far and is still on the eighth fairway but is no longer in the way. (Photograph property of Ted Porter.)

Stylish golfers playing the course in the 1920s. (Photograph property of Ted Porter.)

The call to serve. Worthington men served their country in World War II as they had in previous wars. Here are Ray and Helen Magargal, Helen's sister Eloise Bartlett, and "Brownie" Harold Brown. The child is Joan Osgood Donovan. (Photograph property of Helen Magargal.)

A war memorial. A tribute to those who fought was established in 1947 on the common between the town hall and the First Congregational Church. (The truck belonged to Lawrence "Laurie" C. Mason.) Four crosses bear the names of those whose lives were lost in the two World Wars: William Coffee, Donald Mollison, Norman Eddy, and Russell Shaw. (Photograph property of Ted Porter.)

The result of a generous benefactor. Ground was broken on August 17, 1914, for the library. It was named for Frederick Sargent Huntington, a beloved minister of the Worthington First Congregational Church. Upon his death from typhoid fever at thirty-six, Huntington left his entire estate to the town for the purpose of building a library. (Photograph property of Helen Magargal.)

Dedication. The new library building was dedicated on September 2, 1915, as witnessed by a large crowd of residents. (Photograph property of Helen Magargal.)

Centennial of General Lafayette's visit to Worthington, June 13, 1925. When Pearce's Tavern was on this site, Lafayette spent the night and met with townspeople when traveling from Albany to Boston. Those who attended the celebration at the library dressed in the style of the early 1800s. This child is Mary Burr Hitchcock, who is now a resident of the Maples Senior Housing. (Photograph property of Helen Magargal.)

Also in attendance at the commemoration were Dr. and Mrs. Harlan Creelman (nee Josephine Rice). Mrs. Creelman's grandfather, Colonel William Rice, led a party of men to bring Lafayette into town from Peru. The Creelman home was next to the library. It is now the home of Sandy and Bob Epperly. (Photograph property of Helen Magargal.)

A sportsman's pursuit. Fishing and hunting have always been popular activities in this rural community. Deer were plentiful, though it would appear from this photograph that the raccoon population might be down. Local sportsmen organized the rod and gun club in 1946. Its building, pavilion, and ball field on Dingle Road are used for many events. (Photograph property of Helen Magargal.)

Coon and Turkey Supper. This culinary spectacular was held about fifty years ago at the town hall. Pancake breakfasts, sugar eats, and dinners with town meetings were regular events. Some of those waiting to be served here are (on the far right, from front to back) Ernest Thayer, Lena Thayer, Len Tufts, Doris Tufts, Stanley Mason, Ralph Smith, Madeline Smith, and three unidentified persons; (looking at the camera) Henry Snyder. In the second row from right, second from front, Fred Emerson, (two unknown), Eleanor Porter, Janice Porter and Dan Porter. (Photograph property of Barbara and Ken Pease.)

Teacher Arthur Capen and students at the Ringville School on Ring Road, early 1900s. Mr. Capen was also the church organist and the town librarian for more than sixty years. The building is now the home of Shirley Rida. (Photograph property of Worthington Historical Society.)

Outside Lyceum Hall, now Hillside Electronics, June 12, 1935. These children were transported to this location from as far away as West Worthington and Ringville. They are (front row) Earl Robinson, Barent Pease, Ashley Dodge, Kenneth Pease, William Knapp, Edward Ladr, and Morris Pease; (middle row) Howard Mollison, Frederick Dodge, James Knapp, Richard Smith, Ernest Robinson, Edward Wright, Marietta Sweetman, Alice Eddy, and Shirley Sanderson; (back row) Joyce Mason, Milton Parrish, Paul Sweetman, Shirley Packard, Marjorie Bullock (teacher), Helen Wright, Carolyn Ames, Sylvia Eddy, and Connie Larro. (Photograph property of Pete Packard.)

Students of the West Worthington School, January 1939. The school is now the home of Bonnie and Henry Payson. From left to right are (front row) Paul Granger, Lois Shant, Evelyn Wight, Claire Wisner, and Jane Sears; (middle row) Nancy Sears, Harrison Higgins, Doris Smith (teacher), Gladys Wight, June Parish, and Richard Sears; (back row) Ashley Cole, Patty Magargal, George Leighton, Orrin Parish, and Thelma Hathaway. Doris Smith married a local man, as did many of the educated women who came to Worthington to teach. (Photograph property of Doris Smith.)

Bicentennial celebration, 1968. Numerous events were conducted throughout the community. These included a parade, dances, a commemorative church service, concerts, tours, exhibits, and fireworks. The hairy men who competed in the beard-growing contest were, from left to right, (front row) John Modesto, Bert Nugent, Ernie Nugent, and Joe Sena; (middle row) Henry Payson, Harley Mason, Emerson "Emmy" Davis, and Art Rollins; (back row) Courtney Wheeler, Larry Mason, Alan Rida, Win Donovan, Bobby Warysz, and Gary Granger; (Photograph property of Town of Worthington.)

Five
Town of Blandford

Blandford is situated in the westerly part of Hampden County, sheltered in the foothills of the Berkshires, a continuation of the Green Mountains. It is a town known for its scenic beauty and rolling highland.

Settled by the Ulster Scots and the Irish who came from Hopkinton in 1735 and called Glasgow, the town was incorporated in 1741, and to honor Governor William Shirley's ship it was named Blandford.

Blandford was historically an agricultural community, as many of the old towns were. All the necessities for rural living were provided by the settlers, epitomizing the early American way of life.

Blandford still preserves the air of the village and its past social structures. The imposing steeple of the White Church on the hill; the Blandford American Legion Post; the old schoolhouse that is now the Blandford Historical Society; the Porter Memorial Library; Watson Park; the Blandford Country Store, still standing where the original store was built; the Blandford Club, housed in Mrs. Porter's old summer home; and the Blandford Fair all contribute to the small-town charm of our community.

In a tribute to the love and interest of Dr. Plumb Brown and Mr. Sumner G. Wood, we have compiled a pictorial history of the early way of life, a legacy to be treasured and preserved. Dr. Brown's collection of pictures constitutes a foundation of local history for our town. We also must not forget Sumner Wood—a forefather who collected and conserved an early history that makes Blandford's past a reality that will serve to guide us into the future. Specifically, Sumner Wood's historical works on Blandford include *Ulster Scots and Blandford Scouts*, *The Taverns and Turnpikes of Blandford*, *Soldiers and Sailors of the Revolution from Blandford*, and *The Homes and Habits of Blandford*.

Now, with the aid of Dr. Brown and Mr. Wood, we can take a nostalgic walk into the past of the village and wind our way up Main Street, heading west.

Bennett's Livery Stable opposite the Methodist church on Main Street (1890–1900). Currently this property is the summer home of Atkins and Henrietta Blair.

Blandford Center, looking west. The Main Street Library is on the left, and the Blandford Country Store is on the right.

Tavern sign of Samuel Porter. The original tavern sign pictured in *Taverns and Turnpikes* by Sumner Wood is now on display at the Porter Memorial Library.

Doris W. Hayden in costume for the bicentennial celebration, 1935. She is shown attending the old-folks concert wearing a wedding dress about eighty years old. Mrs. Hayden was librarian from 1949 to 1972. She was town historian until her death on September 1, 1996.

The Methodist church on Main Street in Blandford. This building no longer exists.

The Porter Memorial Library. Given to the residents of Blandford in 1892 by Mrs. Josephine E.S. Porter, the library was dedicated in memory of Mrs. Porter's son, Edgar Sheffield Porter. It was endowed with several hundred volumes she brought from New Haven, which she loaned out to both summer guests and residents before the library was built. (From a historical review written by Frances E. deBraal in 1947.)

Frances E. Tiffany deBrall in 1905. She was librarian in Blandford from 1908 to 1948.

Home of Mrs. Frances E.T. deBrall on Main Street in Blandford.

Old Robinson store and house. This store burned down and was rebuilt by Mr. Peebles. The Blandford Country Store still stands on Main Street today and the charm of by-gone days can still be felt.

Blandford and Russell mail and stagecoach *c.* 1900, driven by E.W. Bennett. With the advent of the train to Russell, Blandford's "summer" settlers used the stage to go back and forth to their homes, or used their own buggies.

H.S. Dean store on Main Street in Blandford.

Mountain House on Main Street in Blandford, 1900.

The "New Hotel" on Russell Stage Road in Blandford, *c.*1930. Orrin Sage, proprietor.

The First Congregational Church of Blandford. Our forefathers' social and spiritual life centered around the church. They placed the church on a high hill where it could be seen by all and "the pines" grew to keep it company. In 1985 the white church was listed in the National Register of Historic Buildings. Built in 1822 by Isaac Damon, it is considered a glorious example of nineteenth-century church architecture. It has recently been restored to its former glory as a house of worship amidst the pines.

The Blandford Historical Society. This schoolhouse built in 1845 was restored by the historical society in 1967 through the generosity of Susan E. Tiffany (1890–1960).

The Blandford Fair or the Union Agricultural and Horticultural Society. The first mention of horseracing at the fairgrounds was in 1867, as reported by "a newsman" according to Lynn Anderson's *Blandford Fair History*. The track was then 1/3 mile long.

The Blandford Fox Club. In 1898, a club was formed by the initiative of Mr. Clarence Bates and Mr. Henry Haley. Lawrence Ripley is seen here with his hounds Big Boy, Giddie, and Lady.

The Cook family at the Bates Maple House, 1920.

The Old Blandford Gold Mine. The Blandford Gold and Silver Mining Company was organized on January 15, 1880. The discovery of the mine occurred in 1875. A few gentlemen from Springfield were walking in the hills and came across a rock. They broke off a piece and showed it to some experts. It was ascertained to be a good indication of silver or gold. The land was leased and a vein of gold and silver found. The mine is still visited today. (From the by-laws of the Blandford Gold and Silver Mining Company, 1880.)

Taggart Fund School in Blandford.

Mr. and Mrs. McDonough in front of their home in Blandford.

Chapel of the First Congregational Church on Main Street in Blandford.

Congregational parsonage on Main Street in Blandford.

"The Pines" on the church hill.

A picture of the Reverend and Mrs. S.G. Wood in their buggy.

Blandford Fox Club members after wildcat hunting, *c.* 1932. The men were found warming up at the Blandford Gas Station by a roving photographer. From left to right are Ralph Pomeroy, Dave Ripley, Herb Hart, unknown, Merry Williams, Ira Bates, and Lawrence Ripley.

Six
Town of Middlefield

Middlefield is considered to be one of the typical hill towns of the county, but with several ranges of hills cutting through it from northwest to southeast and many brooks and rivers cutting their way downhill, its vistas and waterfalls are far from typical.

"Middlefield is a very mountainous town, settled in 1773." This notice was taken from the October 28, 1800 *Hampshire Gazette*. In 1773 the first gristmill was built, and Colonel Mack built a cabin home and cleared a small track of land. Others followed and the records show that a town was organized in 1783. At that time the town voted that two days' work be done by each person on the roads in the year ensuing, as part of each settler's town rate. Further, it voted to accept grain for the remainder of the rate, allowing rye at 3¢ per bushel and Indian corn at 2¢. They also voted to give a £3 bounty to anyone "who shall kill a full-grown wolf in town, and one pound ten shillings for killing a young or whelpwolf."

Edward Pease, the son of Eldrige and Persis Ballou Pease. He was born on September 13, 1838. He served in the Civil War from April 1, 1862, to January 2, 1866. After the war he was a merchant in Huntington.

The children of Ralph and Eila Bell (Ralph Jr, Mary Elizabeth, George, and Eila Rosina) in 1923.

Mary Wright is shown here in a studio portrait.

Clark Wright, in a similar shot to the one above.

Azariah Root. Son of Solomon and Anna (Smith) Root, Azariah was born on February 3, 1862, in Middlefield. He married Anna Mayo Metcalf on April 30, 1887, and lived in Oberlin, Ohio. He was librarian of Oberlin College and a president of the American Library Association.

Ambrose Loveland (Captain Loveland), son of Pain and Phebe (Graves) Loveland. Ambrose was born on August 23, 1896, and died on December 10, 1880. He married Ludy B. Cone (1796–1867), the daughter of Cyrus and Ludy Cone.

The house built by Dr. William Coleman that was later known as Cranberry Lodge. This photograph was taken *c.* 1860.

The Middlefield Congregational Church on the main road. Early records show that the first church was begun in 1783. Meetings were held at private houses and in barns until 1791, when a meetinghouse was finally built.

Robert Stanley Pease, son of Arthur and Lura (McElwain) Pease. He was born on February 26, 1897. He enlisted in World War I on May 31, 1918, at Fort Banks, Massachusetts, and served with the 19th CO. Boston. He was honorably discharged on March 26, 1919 at Fort Banks, MA.

"The Middlefield Boys Brigade." From left to right are as follows: (front row) Luke Bernie, Henry Curley, Mr. Coe, Amasa Granger, and Cecil Alderman; (middle row) Roland Pease, Richard Waite, Paul Nickerson, Russell Ferris, and Merrick Starkweather; (back row) Joseph Kelley, Ralph Bell, Ralph Pease, Reverend Estabrook, Elias Lyman, and Harold Pease.

"The Cook of Hesslewood," Lura McElwain Pease. The photograph was taken by John Storms *c.* 1910.

"The Farmer of Hesslewood," Arthur D. Pease. The photograph was taken by John Storms *c.* 1910.

The Blizzard of '58. Snow covered the Middlefield Congregational Church practically to the roofline.

Bell (Blossom) Corner in 1958. Those who live in Middlefield know it well.

View of the Westfield River Valley from a Middlefield pasture, taken on June 16, 1935, by C.E. Alderman, Middlefield. A local historian wrote of Middlefield in 1879: "It is now one of the finest rural villages among the mountain towns of Hampshire County. Located on a commanding eminence, the view embraces a wide extent of surrounding country, hills and valleys stretching away, a mingled and varying landscape of rocky heights and gentle slopes, steep declivities and smiling meadows, cultivated fields and wood-crowned summits, while beyond all, and partially encircling all, is the blue line of distant mountains." (*A History of Western Massachusetts*, Volume 1, 1926.)

Main Street in Middlefield Center. The post office was established in 1811.

Cecil Alderman, *c.* 1950. The growing season is short in Middlefield, but Cecil still managed to produce prize vegetables. There are pieces of land in this town still being worked by current-day descendants of early settlers. The town suffered greatly in 1874 when a chain of dams gave way, demolishing the old clothing, woolen, and turning mills that had been built up in the middle of the 1800s.

The town of Middlefield's honor roll citing those who served in World War II (1941–1945).

Kenfred Root and Adelia Alderman, married in a high meadow ceremony on October 2, 1937. From left to right are F. Snow Root (best man), Kenfred Root and Adelia, Helen Alderman (matron of honor), and Cecil Alderman (who gave the bride away).

"Sumner Crane holds the horses." This wood-shod sled was used to haul the milk from Ralph Bell's farm to the center during the "Great Snow Storm" of February 1958.

Cecil Alderman, gathering sap from his sugar bush on Alderman Road. This photograph was taken on March 18, 1966, and printed in *The Berkshire Eagle*. Maple sugar production has long been considered a small industry in the town. Sugaring in Middlefield lasts about four to five weeks, from the first of March until mid-April. It has to be above 40 degrees during the day, with freezing nights. The faster you turn the sap into syrup, the better quality product you will get. It takes between 32 and 40 gallons of sap to make 1 gallon of syrup. In 1910, syrup was $1.30 per gallon. In 1978 it was $12 to $15 per gallon. In 1997, syrup sold for an average of $36 per gallon. The rock maple tree has to be 12 inches in diameter or bigger to run good. You can put four or five buckets on each tree. It was said that Clarkson Smith frequently produced 7,000 pounds of maple sugar annually in his handsome sugar bush.

Seven

Town of Huntington

Huntington is located in the southern tier of towns in Hampshire County, southwest from Northampton. The east branch of the Westfield River flows through the entire length of the town north to south. Before the corps of engineers built the Knightville and Littleville Dams, the force of the river during a flood brought great damage to the villages and towns downstream.

The township was number nine in the series ordered by the general court on June 2, 1762. Dr. J.G. Holland's history states, "a native American family by the name of Rhoda Rhoades made the first settlement in 1760, about two miles above the Pitcher Street Bridge on the Westfield River, and was a doctor who died here in 1841 at the age of 90." Others discredit the statement, but it is clear that from 1773 on, a steady stream of settlers came into the area. The Town of Murrayfield was incorporated on October 31, 1765, and included the territory of Norwich. On March 26, 1855, M. Copeland reported that Norwich was asked to consider changing its name to "Huntington." Mr. Huntington was a lawyer from Northampton who, tradition has it, offered his namesake to the town in exchange for a $100 donation toward the foundation of a public library.

On March 10, 1856, the town accepted the creation of a school committee and for the time being also made the school committee members the virtual trustees of the library. The library was kept in Myron L. Church's store. The store burned about 1859, and the library went with it. In later years, the library was located in the Murrayfield School, which burned in 1940. The present library is located on the site of the old Huntington High School.

The Park House at the end of the town park, where the post office is today. This handsome building burned in 1920. Built in 1780, it was one of the oldest buildings in town, called variously Park Tavern, Park Hotel, and Park House. (Photograph property of Huntington Historical Society.)

Inside the Park House when Mr. John Chaplin owned it. (Photograph property of Huntington Historical Society.)

The influence of the railroad. The Boston and Albany began service to Huntington in 1841, bringing more than industrial growth to the area. A postcard from Jeff Penn's collection reads: "Hello everyone. We are up in the mountains for four days with friends. It's just beautiful here." The railroad also provided rural citizens with an important social contact. From the diary of a Norwich housewife, Hannah Bartlett, dated November 15, 1895: "Today we packed our trunks. Grandmother leaves to spend the winter in Prescott [MA]. Cora will meet us in Westfield and ride as far as Boston. I am stopping at Springfield to visit Aunt L." (Photograph property of Huntington Historical Society.)

Coming to Pisgah. Shown here are Thomas Hunter (in the arms of Marion Thomas Hunter), Katherine R. Loomis (in arms of Edith Thomas Loomis), Miriam Hunter Dickinson, and Edward Francis Loomis. In the front row are Nancy Ann Loomis (age six), Miriam Hunter (age three), and George Williston Loomis (age seven). The Dodge car belongs to E.F. Loomis.

A bygone era on Main Street, near the building now housing the Country Journal. From left to right are (front row) Plush Dugas, Ed Hayden, Joe Hewitt, Charley Stanton, and unknown; (middle row) Phil Lafond and G. Tindell (?); (back row) G. Lafond, John Stookins, Tim Bachand, Joe Conroy, and Sam Pero (in window). (Photograph property of Huntington Historical Society.)

The Williams Mill. This was located opposite Moltenbreys Market *c.*1890. The man standing on the wagon was Mr. Bradley. From left to right are unknown, Mr. Gladwin, George Beals, and Mr. W.P. Williams. (The Grace Wheeler Collection.)

Searles Road looking north in the year 1900. The earliest business point in town was Norwich Hill. The area shown is located in the northern part of the village, where there were mills, shops, a schoolhouse, and a post office. (Photograph property of Huntington Historical Society.)

The Giddings and Bartlett Homestead on the corner of Pond Brook Road and Pisgah Road. Southampton historian Mr. Samuel Wright (*Historic Homes of Southampton*) writes: "William K. Bartlett married Hannah, daughter of Harvy Giddings, Norwich, and lives on the farm there. This is a very rocky farm, and the rocks that Mr. Bartlett has blasted and laid in immense walls, one of them 30 feet thick, will quite likely remain as his monument for centuries to come." (Photograph taken by the Howes Brothers on June 13, 1900.)

The Norwich Covered Bridge, shown in the late 1800s. (Photograph property of Huntington Historical Society.)

Huntington Park, c. 1800. (Photograph property of Huntington Historical Society.)

Downtown Huntington in the late 1920s, depicting the bridge that went out in the flood of 1936. It was replaced by the Robert Cross bridge. (The Grace Wheeler Collection.)

A 1941 sleigh ride to church with Nellie pulling. In the year 1781, there were between fifteen to twenty well-loaded teams driven every Sunday from Pisgah to the Norwich Hill church. Shown from left to right are Catherine "Betty" Bartlett, Shirley Bartlett Pomeroy, Mary Bartlett Fairman, Georgia Harring (summer resident and New Jersey schoolteacher visiting the family), and Ray Bartlett (driving).

Hannah Giddings Bartlett.

Raymond Earl Bartlett, age six. In the background is another view of the Giddings and Bartlett farm, comprised of four chestnut barns, a house (now gone). Where Ray is sitting in 1906 is now covered with woods.

A leisurely ride. In 1917 the first trolley car left Lee for Huntington at 11:45 am, arriving at 1 pm. (Jeff Penn Collection.)

The Hallett boys and little sister, *c.* 1940s. From left to right are Clint Hallett (in his 1929 Model A Ford), Anna and Bobby Hallett (in the *c.* 1913 Model T Ford), and Harold Hallett Jr. (in his 1920 Dodge). This family lived where the Bartos now live on Searle Road.

Mary Bartlett Fairman, age four, at Norwich Lake in 1942.

"The Pisgah Panther." From left to right are Katherine Loomis, Ruth Wood, Edith Loomis, unknown, Edward Loomis, unknown, Russell Hunter, and Marion Hunter.

Chester Paper Company. The arrival of the trains in 1841 sparked industrial growth. A paper mill was built in 1852, followed by the woolen mills of Little and Stanton. The Highland Mills in 1870 made superior grades of flannel. Consolidation and mergers are nothing new. By the year 1824, the majority of these once prosperous mills had ceased to operate. (Jeff Penn Collection.)

Camp Norwich, the Springfield Young Men's Christian Association Camp. This was the oldest co-educational camp in the country, opened *c.* 1908. After over ninety years in operation, the camp has closed. Its morning bugle call and evening taps are silent. The site was purchased in 1996 by Springfield College. (Jeff Penn Collection.)

August 1929. Ed Cady of Goss Hill Road enjoys a rare vacation with his second wife, Alma (Pomeroy) Cady, and her mother, Sarah (Bodurtha) Higgins, at the Presque Isle, Maine, home of Arthur and Bessie Higgins. Ed Cady ran Fern Croft Farm on Goss Heights for many years, and the Goss Hill area is still home to several generations of Cadys.

Downtown Huntington in the late 1920s. The Park Cafe and a gas station have replaced the Park House. The Park Cafe blew up, killing John Diamond, proprietor. (The Grace Wheeler Collection.)

Pond Brook. Just below the pond was a mill for grinding bark, run by Seth Porter from 1830 to 1840. Porter also had a tannery. Near it was an ancient gristmill, owned and run for many years by Whitman Knight. The building was afterward turned into a factory that made whip stocks. There also stood a wheelwright shop nearby. Just below was the well-known axe-making establishment of Caleb Hannum, an old affair and quite celebrated from 1815 to 1825. Caleb W. Harvey succeeded him at his death in 1825. They continued the business there until they removed it to Huntington Village about 1845. Moses Hannum continued the business for several years. Half a mile below the Hannums' on Pond Brook was the sawmill of Willard White. Somewhat below there was a cider mill in later years. (Jeff Penn Collection.)

Norwich Hill. In 1773, Norwich Hill became a separate district in Division #9, and by 1781 a church had been built. The present white steepled church on the hill was built in 1841. The residences clustered around the church that once belonged to the Kirkland, Knight, and Hannum families are now the homes of the Knox, Kellem, and Sturgil families. (Jeff Penn Collection.)

The Moore House, now the Huntington Country Store, built in the late 1700s. (Photograph property of Huntington Historical Society.)

The River Breeze, owned and operated by Guy and Cora Barr, in the late 1940s. The establishment was located by Norwich Bridge. (The Grace Wheeler Collection.)

The Bridge Store, an official posting place for special and annual Town Meetings. Folks have gathered at the store for many years to pick up the news, the paper, and some fishing bait. Martin Nichols has been running the Bridge Store since 1984.

Fibber Magee and Molly at the Rapids Cafe on Route 112 in the late 1920s. Molly is on the left, and Fibber Magee is on the far right. (Jeff Penn Collection.)

On Norwich Lake, *c.* 1936. (Jeff Penn Collection.)

Norwich Lake, showing the Massassoit Hotel, 1904. After the hotel burned, the area on the east side of the lake became Camp Laurel, which closed *c.* 1965. (Jeff Penn Collection.)

Current view of Carmelwood, built in 1860 by Horace Taylor as a wedding gift for his daughter. The home is now owned by Katheryn and Fred Corrigan, who have restored and expanded the gardens and provide a bed and breakfast service to the area.

Mrs. Gladys Fredericks in front of the Bartletts' home on Pisgah Road, winding up to throw a snowball, early 1950s. The property is now owned by Pam and Bruce Anderson.

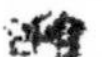

The Murrayfield School. The first Murrayfield School, built in 1892, burned in 1940. The second Murrayfield School, with a gym/auditorium, burned in 1946. The third Murrayfield School opened in 1949. In 1907, the high school was built. In 1930, the town built an extension on the high school to house the library. The present library is located on the site of the old Huntington High School. (Jeff Penn Collection.)

The town of Huntington honor roll, erected in 1950. (Photograph property of Huntington Historical Society.)